At the Rim

Selected Poems

Bob Johnston

At the Rim

Selected Poems

SANTA FE

Sunstone books may be purchased for educational, business, or sales promotional use.
For information please write: Special Markets Department, Sunstone Press,
P.O. Box 2321, Santa Fe, New Mexico 87504-2321.

Body typeface ► Palatino Linotype
Cover design by Vicki Ahl
Printed on acid free paper

Library of Congress Cataloging-in-Publication Data
Johnston, Bob, 1920-
    At the rim : poems / Bob Johnston.
        p. cm.
    ISBN 978-0-86534-814-1 (softcover : alk. paper)
    I. Title.
PS3610.O3839A87 2011
811'.6--dc22

                        2011015241

WWW.SUNSTONEPRESS.COM
SUNSTONE PRESS / POST OFFICE BOX 2321 / SANTA FE, NM 87504-2321 /USA
(505) 988-4418 / ORDERS ONLY (800) 243-5644 / FAX (505) 988-1025

ACKNOWLEDGMENTS

The following poems, or earlier versions of these poems, first appeared in the indicated journals. Permission to reprint is gratefully acknowledged.

Formalist	The Second Excited State
Iambs and Trochees	Paper Roses Poems Written to Order
Kansas Quarterly	Clear Title Dialogue Redefinition
Light Quarterly	Our Animal Friends The Exorcist
Margie	Epitaph of a Procrastinator Sought Through Prayer and Meditation
Ouroboros Review	Coarse Texture
Pasque Petals	Candlelight Sonatina End of the Drought For Kathleen Ferrier Psychic Bridge Running Water There Are No Birds in Manhattan Too Far, Too High Way Out
Pearl	Guided Tour
Rattle	Double Helix Finished Symphony Hazel, South Dakota The Entropy Drag Vanishments Waiting
Riverrun	Mulberry Time The Best Colors Are Mixed The Green Underworld
The Lamp-Post	The Seven Deadly Colors
The Lyric	At the Rim Bedrock
Transcendent Visions	Resting Place Ten Pounds of Beauty

CONTENTS

THE SEVEN DEADLY COLORS

GONE

DOWN

PREFACE

In ninety years of residence on this planet, I have accumulated a lot of inner debris. Most of it is trash, but I have to believe that some of it is worth exposing to public view. These poems are about love, loss, and gratitude, along with some outrage at having been propelled into a century I don't understand at all.

I am particularly grateful to those who helped me along the way to becoming a poet: Joyce Davis, Richard Schramm, Valerie Martínez, Stellasue Lee. I am also grateful to my three children, who have managed to become good people in spite of me. And finally, this book is my farewell to everyone I lost along the way.

I dedicate these poems to my wife, Mary Sue Doyle Johnston, who gave me my first incentive to enter the world of poetry.

—Bob Johnston
Las Vegas, New Mexico

BACK

HAZEL, SOUTH DAKOTA

I

Just before sunset on the first day of May
a small breeze came down from the hills,
loitered in my back yard until dark,
then vanished, leaving behind
a faint aroma, a strange sweetness
with a message to me
        from somewhere.

By September I'd forgotten the message,
or maybe I never understood it,
or maybe there was no message at all—
but something had lodged in my head
like a splinter just below the surface,
and I knew I had to go back
        somewhere.

II

The house was just as I remembered it—
Small, white, with a peaked roof; front porch,
tiny lawn, back yard grown up to weeds,
wild plum trees, vines weighting down the fence.
Everything was there, frozen in time
for fifty years, waiting for me
        to return.

Dusty street, cracked sidewalk,
chicken coop, outhouse,
rusty car up on blocks,
rock pile, plowed field.
Everything was there, except
the row of Russian olive trees,
        vanished.

III

The room was waxed and polished,
ready for my first day of school.
Sunlight traced a pattern on the desks,
reflected onto the blackboards
and the map of the United States
and the Palmer Method alphabet
        that circled the room.

I inhaled the odor of blackboards,
old chalk dust and new furniture polish.
An American flag stood in one corner.
The ancient plumbing gave off soft gurgles.
Two flies blundered against a windowpane
in perfect rhythm with the beat of the clock
        we called Big Ben.

Fifty years hadn't changed anything,
not even my beautiful red-haired teacher.
She sat at her desk, disembodied,
floating beneath a halo of sunlight,
book open, ready to read us a story.
I called out "Miss Hennessy," and she smiled
        as she disappeared.

IV

I headed west, homeward bound.

The Russian olives are blooming again,
and their strange aroma drifts down the canyon.
Finally, I know why I went back
to make the connection, to understand
the thread that binds me to the past,
to whenever it all began,
        wherever.

WAITING

It didn't rain all summer, and the wind
Blew yellow dust from Colorado, mixed
With black dirt of our own. Tumbleweeds
And dust had buried all the fences. The taste
Of blackness was always in my throat, and grit
Was in my bed. Toward the end of day
We sat and watched the devils march across
A dirty sunset. There wasn't much to do—
The crops were burned and all the cows had died.
My father said that next week it would rain
Because the Lord would send it. In the north
Dry lightning flashed against a black curtain.

COARSE TEXTURE

You always were an ornery sort of critter
with a crossgrained disposition.
We used to say you'd swallowed too much sand
in those bad years
when you had to ride out to the back range
to see how many head of our herd had choked
on tumbleweeds and dust.

It wasn't until we laid you out in your best suit
when I finally put my hand on your face
that I knew
the sand had gotten into your blood
and kept us apart.

RUNNING WATER

It hadn't rained all summer.
The crops burned out again
and two of our cows died
but winter brought a lot of snow
drifting clear down from Hudson Bay
across the prairie, and it seemed
that maybe just maybe
the drought had ended.

It was still bitter cold in the mornings
but a south wind brought a trace
of spring. Any day now
the robins would arrive.

Down in the back pasture
the snow was piled deep in the gully.
"Yellowbanks," they called it,
but I'd never seen water running
and the nearest river was sixty miles away.
Off in the distance I heard old Wags
barking, but not his rabbit-chasing yip—
this was one I'd never heard before.

There was something else too, a hiss
and gurgle, and it came closer
and turned into a rush of water
snaking over the snow. Wags did his best
to turn it back. He raced along the edge
and snapped and snarled at the water,
then he gave up, sat beside me on the bank
and watched the water run its course.

END OF THE DROUGHT

The rains came last week
and washed the sky clean.
The creek down in the pasture
is running again, tentatively,
as if trying to remember.

I smell the sweet rainy air
and tip my cap to the new moon.
In the east, thunderheads retreat,
catching the last sunlight.

The ground is new-green,
and mayflowers
break their long sleep.

Above the biggest cottonwood tree
two kingbirds zig and zag
connecting the dots
from insect to insect.

In the quiet before cricket-time
I hear the step of a cottontail.
He nose-wobbles through the grass,
then freezes. A dark owl
traces a silent arc.

Crickets sing a verse, and frogs
join the jubilee chorus

THERE ARE NO BIRDS IN MANHATTAN

I remember the emptiness of the land,
The whistling of wind across the plain.
I remember the gold at the setting of sun,
The musty smell of a morning rain.

I remember the mountains, the valiant clouds
Mounting to heaven in a turbulent pile,
The pine and the spruce surviving the storm
With roots planted deep in the rocky soil.

I remember the caldera, the Valle Grande,
A carpet of green in an infinite bowl
With miniature cattle away in the distance,
An island of rock like an ancient troll.

Reality enters, invades the now:
A glass-lined canyon, a river of asphalt,
Exhaust in blue, drizzle in grey.

I look for the sky, but my eyes are burning;
I listen for birdsong, but the birds have gone
South for the winter, west for the century,
Leaving me here in the city, alone.

UP

POEMS WRITTEN TO ORDER

If I could spend a week or two or more
In matching rhymes and meters to the text,
I'd write an epic full of blood and gore
And heroines discreetly oversexed.
The plot would be replete with rue and passion
And daring deeds that could not fail to thrill.
The hero, Rambo dressed in latest fashion,
Would waste the baddies twice—an overkill.
This epic ought to make me rich and famous—
I'll write a movie script beyond compare.
The story's geared for any ignoramus—
Let critics find the message hidden there.
  My epic verses do not meet the test
  And so I'll write a sonnet on request.

OUR ANIMAL FRIENDS

An Alphabestiary

The **ant** is never known to shirk—
In fact, she really loves her work.
But when her turn has come to play,
She goes on picnics every day.

The **beagle** is a droopy hound
With ears that drag along the ground.
His howl would surely be illegal
From anything except a beagle.

The **cow** is useful in her way,
She dines on grass and chews all day,
Delivers milk of any brand
From all four spigots on demand.

The **dinosaur** once ruled the swamp,
The earth resounding to his stomp.
Now he's extinct, the reason plain—
Excessive bulk, deficient brain.

The **elephant** is gray and huge;
He has no need for subterfuge.
Although there's nothing that he fears,
He holds a grudge a hundred years.

The **frog** prefers a home aquatic;
His leaps are truly acrobatic.
His booming bass is quite incredible,
And best of all, his legs are edible.

The **goldfish** is a happy pet.
He'll never sulk and never fret.
Alive, he's easy to maintain;
If dead, just flush him down the drain.

The **hornet** builds a paper shell
And then defends it very well.
He hangs a sign for all to see:
Keep out, you fool, don't mess with me.

If you have seen a big **iguana,**
You've surely seen more than you wanna—
Each one more ugly than his brother,
A face loved only by his mother.

The **jaybird** is a jaunty chap,
Blue-feathered with a pointed cap.
Ten ounces of pure dynamite,
He's always spoilin' for a fight.

The **kangaroo** can leap and bound
To cover miles and miles of ground.
He jumps so high, comes down so slow
His next stop may be Tokyo.

The **leopard** is a spotted cat
With whiskers long and haunches flat.
They say he cannot change his spots—
Why change? He likes his polkadots.

The **mouse** is small and gray and meek,
His voice so weak it's just a squeak.
But he excels at hide-and-seek,
And as a streaker he's unique.

The **nightingale** is born to sing,
But never when she's on the wing.
She's just a sedentary bird,
With a compulsion to be heard.

The **oyster** lives within his shell.
He's him or her, you cannot tell.
But if you irritate the girl,
He'll probably produce a pearl.

The **porcupine's** a mass of quills;
His life is quite devoid of thrills.
When making love he shows restraint—
A sadomasochist he ain't.

The **quail** never thought her name
Would have a nasty sort of fame
Which always scares the randy male:
He hears the phrase "San Quentin Quail."

The **rabbit** is a mass of fears,
Built-in antennas are his ears.
He cannot add, much less subtract,
But multiplying is his act.

The **skunk** a mighty beast is he;
He treads his path with dignity.
He has no foes, he has no friends;
His means will justify the ends.

The **tomcat** loves a friendly fight,
He sleeps all day and roams all night.
He will not tell you where he went,
But smirks and yawns, impenitent.

The **unicorn** has magic powers.
His mane is white, bedecked with flowers.
His magic works with just one horn.
With two horns—superunicorn.

The **vampire** is misunderstood;
He's really out to do you good—
Like old-time surgeons, a believer
That letting blood will cure a fever.

The **weasel** sneaks around at night
To satisfy his appetite.
He leaves behind a bloody mess,
A token of his great success.

The **x-ray fish** can never hide
What all takes place in his inside.
He has no modesty or shame:
For him, digestion is a game.

On his own turf the **yak** is king;
He is the source of everything
The Yakuts need. They never lack
For food or fur. All hail the yak!

The **zebra** wears a striped suit
That hardly qualifies as zoot.
Essentially, he's just a square
Pretending to be debonair.

THE BEST COLORS ARE MIXED

An iron grip is no substitute for a broad brush
when painting a cornucopia or stripes on a tiger.

Your eyes rebel at the sight of a rainbow
stretched out across the canyon to the next mesa.

Everything has a silver cast, if you can only sense it,
but the color can dig in and mask your best word.

The elk on the mesa is gold, and as light as paper,
with lightning-rod antlers and the hoofs of the Devil.

You cannot control what you see, but only plow
every element of your dream back into a colorless void.

Your board is set with linen and silver, but there is no food
on the table and no yellow grain in the barn.

Your purple banners march to their destiny
and the wind eats red dust at the foot of the mesa.

THE ENTROPY DRAG

On the last bus from Hackensack
I am the only passenger, except
two drunks sleeping it off.
We bounce through the suburbs
and down dark roads
to the music of Guy Lombardo.

Thick air drags at the wheels,
the engine overheats
and the bus stops. Lombardo
is flatter than usual. The driver
leaves forever and I'm alone
with snores and stale air and Carmen
singing "When Did You Leave Heaven?"

A blue fog drifts in through the door,
residue of exhaust and mercury lamps.
It envelops us impartially
and brings us to equilibrium
and a final stasis
with snoring
sour melody
and me.

TOTAL IMMERSION

In the ocean we dwell outside time,
no beginning, no end, no regrets,
no theories of heaven or hell,
only infinity and the deep.

We are still intruders, aliens, lung-breathers
passing the time until the transformation
comes to take us beyond the barriers,
into the green phosphorescent world.

In this place where we wait our turn,
the creatures of the ocean
go their way, salute us
as they pass.

FINDING HOME

I've never gone more than fifty miles from my home town which just happens
to be New York, because there never seemed to be any reason to roam,
and anyway I think I've been almost everywhere, or will be.

I found a place once that had everything I wanted, acres of green grass and trees,
a little white house, surrounded by mountains, not too many people.
I'd like to spend the rest of my days there, if I can find it again.

There are a million other places, give or take a few thousand,
where I've been, and not just in my mind. I remember the sounds and the smells,
the color of the clouds, even the feel of the air.

I remember old St. Petersburg, crowded streets, a dirty saloon,
the old drunk Marmeladov spilling his guts to some young punk,
and Sonya with her new yellow ticket, walking the streets.

I was stranded once on a mountain peak, no shelter, bare rock, no place to hide,
with lightning blasts all around me and the smell of ozone and fear,
no way to get home, and oh god the thunder. It ruptured an eardrum.

Another place: Red, everything red with volcano light, smell of brimstone,
tongues of flame, hot lava, gray ash, like the old legend of hell.
The only thing missing was the devil.

Once I was lost on a purple desert under a pale green sun that never set
and wind that sandblasted my skin. The oasis wasn't a mirage, but
the trees were crystal and the pool was mercury.

My last stop was in the Dust Bowl. Fences choked with tumbleweeds
and banked with dust. A dirty sky with dry lightning in the north.
Dead cattle everywhere, but no people.

All these million places run forever on tracks that never meet,
and a few million more places where I've never been,
but I have to try them all.

CLEAR

THE SECOND EXCITED STATE

All the atoms spinning in my head
Were in the ground state, very nearly dead
Or atrophied, without illumination
In unexcited stasis, resignation
To status quo. Incoherent light
Failed to penetrate the grayest night.

But you, the keeper of the laser came
Into my sphere to renovate the flame.
Amplified to stimulate emission
Of radiation, always in transition
From state to state, and always under stress,
Until you quench me, I must fluoresce.

THESE FOOLISH THINGS

Once there was a song
about a cigarette
that bears a lipstick's traces,
a tinkling piano
in the next apartment
and all the foolish things
that remind me of you.

Long ago and almost gone,
you are still there, hidden
in some dim attic, preserved
in uncorrupted flesh,
waiting
for the sign, the reveille
to bring you back in living color
to mock the years between
that never were.

Zorina takes her first two steps onto the stage.
Jo Stafford sings "He's Gone Away."
Koussevitsky raises his baton.
The sun rises over the Atlantic.
The Valkyries ride.
Sam plays it again.

SONG IN FOUR MOVEMENTS

You served in F-sharp, and the ball
was uncommonly yellow, too bright
to return.

You left the board and hovered
at apogee, a red arrow ignoring
gravity.

We lay on fluorescent grass and watched
uncertain clouds whirl and sharpen
their edges.

No one else came to share the night,
but lightning strobes illuminated
our dance.

QUARTET

The pitch zeroes on perfection
as they tune, scrape their feet
and cough. No smiles, for this
is serious business, black and white
with little room for error.

They make their statement. The music
moves them forward and now they are
the music and the black notes
spin out a single filament
that never ends. The cellist smiles.

SOUGHT THROUGH PRAYER AND MEDITATION

With you I have known peace, Lida, and
now you say you're going crazy.
—James Thurber

He talks to God each morning and evening
and sometimes in between, on his lunch hour,
for he is a righteous man and is guided by the Word
as revealed to him directly in these conversations.

God has told him he must be a stern and loving husband,
that he must instruct me in the proper duties of a wife,
because I am of an inferior species that never can aspire
to the Priesthood. Such is the word of God and Saint Paul.

My duties are to love and cherish and obey, particularly
to obey, to serve him at his pleasure and to bear many children,
to keep a clean house and cook nutritious meals and iron his shirts
and those of our children, who will all be boys.

God has told him that the Ten Commandments
are only the beginning, that he must always seek
direct instruction on how to regulate his household
for maximum comfort and the greater glory of God.

I wanted to talk direct to God too, so today I tried,
and I think I made a connection, but Her advice
did not really make any sense, because all I heard was
Sharpen the icepick and wait.

LORETTO CHAPEL

1.

Sister Ellen crossed herself and climbed the ladder
To the choir loft—it seemed higher than Mount Sinai.
She closed her eyes and prayed to God to be forgiven
For her fear and for her muttered imprecations
Upon the architect, whose only god was order
And symmetry. Really, they should have a staircase.
Every night for seven weeks she offered prayers
To Saint Joseph. He would understand the problem.
Breathing hard, she reached the loft and laid her dustcloth
On the railing while she rested. Mother Agnes
Often said the ladder was God's will, but then—
Mother Agnes didn't have to climb the ladder.
Sister Ellen started. She must have been dozing.
The chapel door was open wide, and in the sunlight
Stood a stranger, a tall man with a wooden toolbox.
He set the toolbox down and smiled at Sister Ellen,
Then he pointed to a corner by the choir loft
And traced a spiral with his finger: *Room aplenty.*

2.

Sister Martha gently nudged the last visitor
Out the door, and locked it. Tonight she was lonely,
Missing the Sisters and the school and the convent—
All were gone. Only she remained, and the chapel.
She had told the story of the miraculous staircase
To nine thousand two hundred twenty tourists—some believers—
How an unknown carpenter appeared, in answer
To the Sisters' prayers. He labored for seven weeks,
Hewed and soaked and bent and planed and pegged and polished
Each piece of wood. The staircase, seeming unsupported,
Spiraled from the floor. Then, when it was finished,
He disappeared, and never came to ask for payment.
Sister Martha climbed the staircase to the choir loft.
She dusted all the benches, though they didn't need it,
And sat, thinking of the chapel and the ladder
As they were when Sister Ellen sat there, dozing.
It seemed that any minute now the door would open,
The carpenter would smile at her: *Room aplenty.*

3.

Sister Rita flicked a speck of dust from the staircase,
Stood back and admired it—burnished wood glowing,
Strange and foreign grains, in two full turns it spiraled
Upward. An engineering marvel, so the guidebook called it.
Last June, the scientists had brought their instruments,
Photographed and probed the staircase. She watched them closely,
Making sure they didn't harm it. Tonight, the chapel
Was ready for a wedding. Poinsettias dripped below
The Stations of the Cross; the walls were wreathed with holly
And piñon branches. She felt that she was truly blessed—
The Lord had chosen her as guardian of the chapel
When he gathered Sister Martha to His bosom.
Sister Rita thought the ceremony was beautiful
Even though the groom wore jeans, and the priest
Was an Episcopalian. She kissed the bride and told her
She knew they would be happy, because they had been married
With the staircase as a witness, and the carpenter
Had told Sister Ellen there was *room aplenty.*

BEDROCK

The words of love come easily. They sound
As empty as a shell within a dream
That echoes noise more random than profound,
Galactic symphonies without a theme.
The deeds of love are hard to do. They seem
Routine, prosaic, far too commonplace
To fit into the universal scheme
Of love. But kindness makes a better case
For love than hollow valentines with ragged lace.

REDEFINITION

If you could read the words I never wrote
Because a poet wrote them long ago,
You'd learn about magnanimous despair
And parallels of love that never meet.
But even words that sound a graceless note
Or verses that are hardly apropos
To such a lofty subject may prepare
A way for love until it is complete.
And so I write in tepid metaphors,
Compare your beauty to a budding rose,
And search for words and songs of troubadours
To tell you what your heart already knows.
  Although the stars oppose, our love will find
  Conjunction of the body and the mind.

DARK

THE EXORCIST

His tools were simple—
two paring knives and a drill.
He said it might hurt a little
but I'd feel a lot better
with my skull ventilated.

He wore a ski mask and brown gloves,
which seemed a little irregular,
but his confidence convinced me.
He gave me two shots of whiskey
and went to work.

The operation was a success
and all of the evil spirits left,
but now two English sparrows
are building a nest inside
and the noise keeps me awake.

IN MEMORIAM

The row of shin bones in my garden
marks the graves of predecessors
color-coded to show the mode of death
red for murder   green for suicide
        yellow for accidents

Down the road is a large puddle
and one shin bone properly tagged
as male white forty-five
six feet two   two hundred pounds
        no identifying marks

He came this way thinking the road
went east for nearly forever
or left or right or possibly
in a parabolic curve   or great circle but
        it stopped here

The tag is blue to indicate
he did not meet a violent death
but kept on running east
until he stopped to rest   and promptly
        deliquesced

Before the rains come tonight
and wash away the puddle
I'll retrieve the shin bone
and paint it blue   a nice touch
        for my garden

THE GREEN UNDERWORLD

Here is a gathering of drowned corpses:
Sailors, fishermen,
Titanic passengers.

They have all assembled here
drawn against their will
by a call to seek their own.

Unravaged by sharks or decay,
they stand as if suspended by wires,
their feet just off the bottom.

They sway gently with the current
and try to communicate with mermaids,
who ignore them.

DOUBLE HELIX

The road leads downward, away from reality,
a giant ramp for a parking garage,
a bobsled run packed with snow,
turns unreasonably banked,
an infinite spiral.

The transcendent bobsled skids
onto a frigid plain covered with six feet of snow,
an Eskimo hell.

The city is laid out in neat icy squares,
unpopulated on this Saturday night.
All the fantastic citizens have gone to the mall,
the center of everything bright and beautiful,
three miles across, yellow and red brick,
snack bars, kiosks, stores, rest rooms,
but no exits.

Each rest room is four-dimensional,
an intricately coiled inner ear that leads back
to the beginning. Pollution slithers
from the snack bars onto the store fronts,
a gigantic two-dimensional movie set
populated by extras with frozen feet
and nondimensional faces.

At the very center of the mall, an iron staircase
spirals upward into the fog, a trail
back to reality. But the staircase is not
miraculous: At first touch it crumbles
into a heap of red rust.

TERMINATION

Today began like any other day.
The sun rose reluctantly, and the magpies
swore at each other. The freeway noise
was muffled by the mist. Across the valley
the Sandia peaks radiated an artificial red.
The air had a seasonable bite
as it descended from the canyon.

The day was completely average, in fact
a little boring. Then just before noon
     the pattern broke
     the last leaf fell
from the aspen in the back yard
and as it struck the hollow ground
a cloud appeared at the top of Mount Olympus,
larger than a man's hand but not by much.
It spread from peak to peak across the valley
bringing thunder and lightning and sleet and snow
but not a breath of wind. The cloud pressed down
on the just and unjust alike, smothering all motion.
Traffic halted and power failed and streets groaned
as blackness descended on the longest afternoon.

Then a great wind came out of the west
out of the mouth of the sun.
It shredded the clouds into bite-size fragments
and stacked them in polished tiers.

This sunset has lasted forever
or at least up to now.
The sun stands still
not for battle, but to reinvent
shades of red
and harmonics of the spectrum.

A DAY LATE

I

in a motel somewhere
in texas on a tuesday probably
fog leaks in and crouches on the ceiling
waits for me to make a move

gut lightning prods me to the floor
scrabbling from bed to dresser
for a bottle that isn't there

outside a dove monotones
your fault

II

the clocks have stopped at eight
on a wednesday morning and the refrigerator
apologizes before it dies

a cockroach rattle in the wastebasket
crescendos and fades without an echo
the house settles with a sigh
ice crystals fall from the ceiling

somewhere a dove monotones
your fault

THE TIE THAT BINDS

Phantoms of the eyeballs come and go,
Red shapes upon my corrugated world.
Distorted shadows of the past recall
the knots of fear that were my daily bread,
the burning cross of righteousness and hate
that drove away the only one who cared.

Bound by broken promises and vows
and drunken dreams and longing unfulfilled,
I try to snap the one thin strand that holds
me to the earth.
Let me float away.

THE TRACK TO NOWHERE

I never had time to stop for Death. He hasn't called my name or shouted "Halt," but I can feel his acid breath on my back. I hurtle through swamps and forests and burning bushes, pulled by a mighty magnet called Paradise, Valhalla, The Gardens of Delight. Rosebushes tear at my arms, and their perfume hangs in my nostrils like the vapor from a corpse. The path narrows, roughens, darkens, as I tunnel into a blur of swirling white. I am afraid to see beyond the blur, afraid to look back at the darkness. There is no escape, no more running. I will stop and wait.

Please wait with me.

THE SEVEN DEADLY COLORS

PURPLE

I was featured in last September's issue of *Fortune.*
They called me one of the power brokers of the world,
told how I am the power behind the throne at Dupont,
Microsoft, Exxon, and General Motors, not to mention
Big Tobacco, Disney, and the American Presidency itself.
They photographed me at work, at play, and at home
in my castle. And the photographs came out fairly well,
although all in all, I think they hardly did me justice.
Also, the article failed to mention the fact
that I have not lost touch with my humble beginnings,
that I am still very much a commoner.

After a series of calamities that stripped me of
my rank, my title, my privileges,
my fortune, my wife, my good name,
I still find myself entirely willing to admit
that I am the foremost citizen of the world
who receives welfare checks.

GOLD

It is a comfort to know that I
will never be completely destitute
because Uncle Heinrich left me
some valuable souvenirs
from Auschwitz including
some that he personally
extracted from the Jews
now in my safe deposit box
as insurance against a rainy day
not that I expect to go bankrupt
in the immediate future
but you never know
what might happen
in these uncertain times
even though I have prospered
and bought up most of the property
in this city and hold mortgages
on the rest and the only thorn
in my side is that bastard
Cliffordson my next door neighbor
whose house is bigger than mine
and he laughs in my face
when I offer him twice
what the house is worth
but I will get him yet
squeeze him out of his business
tie up all his assets
ruin his reputation
then he will have to sell
at my price.

RED

Leroy is big and black and ugly
uncultured and definitely homosexual
but he's never made a pass at me
in the two weeks I've been in here.
He's not really a bad sort but thank god
I'm not a pervert like him.

I tried to explain it all
how I was driven to follow my star
till it led me to the holy grail
the perfect innocence and love
but why did I think he'd understand
when nobody understands?

He pulled a knife from under his mattress
homemade shiny wicked.
Make love to this, you son of a bitch
any day now.

My first loves were sixteen
but they were a disappointment
too long in the world still beautiful
but innocence all gone.

Through an extensive test program
I established that the ideal age is two
completely uncorrupted
innocent but oh so aware!

My last love was not yet two
a shiny angel face golden curls
and in her last minute
like the others
she really loved me.

BLACK

I am the leading authority on fossils of the Upper Jurassic,
author of twelve books and two hundred ten scientific papers.

As the invited lecturer at the annual meeting
of the American Geological Society, I was reporting
on my discovery of a previously unknown fossil, a new species
of trilobite that I have named, appropriately, after myself.

In the question period after the lecture, I modestly received
the kudos so generously bestowed by my peers.
But then that pipsqueak Manning, a johnny-come-lately
without tenure or reputation, had the audacity
to question my finding, to suggest that my fossil
came from deposits a mere million years old.

The blackness descended.

I endured his blithering sarcasm
and the questioning looks of my peers.
I defended my position with all the skill
and authority of my forty years in the profession,
and judging by the applause, I think I had convinced
everyone who was worth convincing.

Finally the session was over.
To show there were no hard feelings
I invited Manning to my room
for a drink and some friendly discussion.

I ended the discussion
with a knife between his ribs.

And it was good.

PUCE

My weekly column runs in fifty papers
and my book *Your Roving Gourmet*
has sold two million copies.

My palate is a finely tuned instrument
that never makes a mistake on a vintage
or fails to identify the source of caviar.

When I enter a restaurant, the maître d'
snaps to attention, and the staff is alerted
to cater to my every whim.

I partake sparingly of every course,
cleansing my palate with sorbet
between courses. I sip each wine.

It is a good life, and I have no complaints.
But of late I find myself going forth, incognito,
to seek out dingy all-you-can-eat buffets.

Tonight it was a Mexican buffet.
I went through the line three times
for double helpings of tamales and enchiladas.

On my way home, I was suddenly stricken
with nausea, and vomited on the sidewalk
of the restaurant I had reviewed yesterday.

GREEN

Gabe was three years older than me
but he had no use for books
so we were in the same grade.
Momma was always after him:
"Gabe, why can't you be more like your brother?"

I finished high school a year early
with nine offers of scholarships
including Harvard. It was a breeze
and I was *summa cum laude.*

Gabe dropped out when he was fifteen,
got his girl friend pregnant,
did a couple of years in juvie
for stealing an airplane.

I started up my own company
with a little capital from my father,
and we were there at the right time.
In ten years we were a *Fortune 500.*

He worked the drilling rigs for two years.
Then he got onto Red Adair's crew,
snuffed fires and capped off blowouts
from Afghanistan to Zanzibar.

When the war came along,
I was called to Washington
as a special adviser to the President
to coordinate the defense industry.

Gabe joined the Marines early on.
He saw it all, from Pearl to Okinawa.
He came back loaded with medals
and an eye patch.

I've been married fifty years
to my childhood sweetheart.
The children all turned out well:
Astronaut, doctor, physicist.

Gabe never married. He always said
women are where you find them
but the best of all are in Iran
once you get behind the veils.

I didn't plan to get into politics,
but everything fell into place.
Governor, senator, and then
Ambassador to France.

We heard from him once in a while.
Shooting scrapes, a bank robbery,
a plot to blow up the Glen Canyon dam,
a couple of prison terms.

Life is winding down for me.
I spend my days writing my memoirs.
At Christmas, all the clan gathers,
four generations, still closely knit.
I am reasonably healthy,
have my own teeth
and shoot in the 90s.

His last hurrah was spectacular.
He highjacked a load of plutonium
on its way to Los Alamos.
Things went wrong, a guard was killed.
Gabe headed for the hills.
He held out for two weeks in a cave,
till they starved him out and shot him.

It's been a good life, and I have no regrets,
but God, how I wish I'd had his.

GRAY

The world outside my window is grimy
with fog dripping from tired trees.
The window has never been washed
and all the dirt is on the inside.

There is work to be done,
poems to write, books to read.
I sit at my supercomputer
and play solitaire.

Two flies are trapped in a web
woven by a weary spider.
I kneel before the telly
and worship the faded colors.

GONE

AT THE RIM

When you were here the summer fruit was ripe
And love could stay without a robe or tent.
The morning sun fell softly on our sleep,
A yellow wash for pleasures still undreamt.

But then you passed all boundaries of light
Into a darkness that you call your own.
The autumn leaves have faded while I wait
And winds are blowing cold against the sun.

CLEAR TITLE

The last time you were here
I had ten oil wells with no dry holes
a castle with fifty rooms and a moat
stocked with alligators
not to mention
a direct pipeline to the almighty.

Now I have a goldfish
a bristlecone pine two thousand years old
three rooms and bath
several mountains complete with clouds
forty-two symphonies
and a chess set made of everlasting plastic.
They'll all be here
in case you come this way again.

DIALOGUE

We faced each other through the glass.
Without the beard he looked smaller
and the gray shirt sagged
on his shoulders. He seemed
to be growing backward,
and I wondered if he
would become
a little boy again
with blond hair.

He said the food was okay
and I told him the frost
hadn't hurt the peaches
and his mother sent her love.

We went on talking
until the glass clouded
with the years between.

PSYCHIC BRIDGE

You dealt the cards and bid
one spade without looking,
then bid one spade again,
insisting, "Surely I am worth
at least one spade
to dig a grave."

My daughter who was lost
and now is lost again,
how can I help you?
My hand is weak.

You tore the ace of spades in half
and asked if you could be excused.

They brought us a new deck.

PAPER ROSES

It was just one of those things,
Just one of those crazy flings
—Cole Porter

We never thought that our affair would last,
But here we are, one year right to the day.
We hardly realized the time had passed
While neither you nor I have walked away.
We said that we were children of our age—
With no commitment, free to come and go,
No solemn vows, no signatures, no cage,
Just freedom, love, and lots of room to grow.
But now you tell me that we've reached the end:
"So wonderful—until we grew apart."
We're civilized. I'll always be your friend
And hang around in case you change your heart.
    I'll play it cool and say it's no big deal
    While waiting, waiting for the hurt to heal.

WANDERING MERMAID

We might have missed each other
by a few decades or light-years
but the tide washed us ashore,
dropped us into a small pool.

We survived. The tide came in,
carried us out to sea,
divergent and unwilling,
destinations unknown.

Now, from my home on dry land
I hear of your journeys,
how the ocean
is your home.

You play with dolphins,
migrate with whales,
fight with giant squid,
rule in Atlantis.

When I listen to a seashell
I hear your alien voice
telling me you remember
the tidal pool.

VISITOR

For a little while
you lighted our sky.
Primitives, we stood in awe.

Now your path leads
somewhere beyond the sun.
We cannot follow.

Return, return!
Some of us may still be here.

FOR KATHLEEN FERRIER

You have gone away, and the house is empty.
Once it was full of children. You sang to them
quiet songs of flowers, magic silver bells,
            a small waterfall.

We listened to your voice and heard a promise
of birth, awakening, newly budded trees,
apple wine, white light that flooded far beyond
            the distant planets.

Now you are all gone. We are left
with a slender legacy, a distant echo,
a voice from a phonograph, mourning
            in *Kindertotenlieder.*

On that wild and stormy night
when our children heard the call,
why did you follow them
            into the dark forest?

AURORA

I looked for you at midnight
when the stars were too thick to stir.

You promised to come to me
as soon as you gathered the lights
and arranged them in your hair.

I looked for you when a cloud
moved quietly over the moon.

FINISHED SYMPHONY

My first twenty years I'd never heard an honest-to-God
live symphony, and then I started at the top:
Koussevitsky and his Boston combo,
Carnegie, Wolfgang's G minor.
When those first notes hit, they lifted me out of my seat,
floated me somewhere above the proscenium,
where I stayed for the next two weeks.
I can still hear those notes.

The slow movement was from Brahms. The violins spun it out
into a single white filament that looped over my head
and back to the stage. I tried to hold onto it,
but it slipped through my fingers.

Instead of a minuet we had Ellington. This was early Ellington,
before he got delusions of grandeur. The mood was indigo
and the stage rocked in rhythm while the brass growled,
the A-train rumbled under the auditorium
and I danced in the aisle
until they put me out.

The last movement capped the climax with Mahler's Resurrection Symphony.
Naturally, it was too loud, too long, and out of tune. The violins
begged for mercy, and the concertmaster took a swig of water
or possibly gin. The notes heaped up in weary piles,
waiting for the final
molto ritardando.

It ended, with no applause and no encores. The audience was long gone.
I sat alone in the darkened hall, waiting for the lights to come up.
They never did. The conductor disappeared in a puff of smoke
and the weary musicians filed offstage. I clapped and clapped
for an encore, anything
to break the silence.

CANDLELIGHT SONATINA

When last we said goodbye in candlelight,
Your face was luminous with inner fire,
Unearthly beauty, goddess of the night,
Beyond my utmost aim, beyond desire.
But then you brought me shadows from the moon,
Starflowers with a taste of apple wine.
We sang and soared beneath a red balloon,
We seized the day, completed our design.
The years have passed since last I saw your face;
The weight of time bears down, and we are old.
The magic vanished. Now the commonplace
Spreads through the earth, brings in the cold.
But you, the youthful goddess, will stay with me
So long as one candle lights my memory.

DOWN

RESTING PLACE

This looked like a good place to finish out my days.
Grass, fruit trees, a flowing spring, and privacy.
After a journey of several hundred years, ending yesterday,
I was ready to rest for another century.

In the absolute quiet of the midday sun
I warmed my bones and watched an eagle
perched at the top of a dead oak—
immobile, solid, permanent.

Today I saw the sign on the other side of the clearing:
Dead Animals Prohibited Here. Although I regret
any inconvenience that I may cause, it is too late
to move on. Please don't fence off the spring.

VANISHMENTS

The art of losing isn't hard to master
—Elizabeth Bishop

Mysterious disappearance is the official name that means insurance will refuse to pay
for vanished statuettes or diamond rings or the ordinary daily loss of keys and pens
and checkbook and glasses but these vanishments are not really all that mysterious
since matter is mostly empty space and any slight relaxation of the binding force
will disperse the electrons as a cloud and nuclei as dust that settles out of sight
but when yesterday disappeared the vanishment was much more noteworthy
for even if yesterday was not too memorable it was still twenty-four hours
and its disappearance gave a faint *plop* as air rushed in to fill the vacuum
then a whole year vanished namely 1976 with many events probably
then everything since 1928 leaving only some childhood memories
and the routine of daily life continued as if there were still a past
with eating sleeping laundry shopping rambling conversations
with people who were still here but they sometimes dimmed
and scenes that faded out like mirages or maybe ghosts
of years of long ago or now or years not yet to come
while man and all his works have passed from view
and the landscape once full of streams and trees
is barren and the horizon narrows and now
the sun disappears and then
the moon and stars
and I am alone
on high mesa
naked
afraid

WAY OUT

Lost again in my private wasteland,
a warehouse where old machinery
comes home to die. A crawler tractor
lies on its back, treads spinning.

Steam hisses from the side
of a ruptured boiler,
twisted tubes protruding,
a disemboweled elephant.

Green venom drips from the ceiling,
etches a luminous circle around the tractor.
The treads come to rest with a sigh
and a smell of burned metal.

This is not my home. A red arrow
high on the wall says *Salida*
but it points to no exit, no path,
no highroad to lead me home.

TOO FAR, TOO HIGH

My figures fail to tell me
How far the Village lies—
—Emily Dickinson

I cannot tell how far the village lies
Beyond the ragged mountains in the west.
I came too late to say my last goodbyes.

My pathway leads to red and purple skies,
A flowing spring where I can stop to rest
And ask again how far the village lies.

While looking upward, searching for the prize,
I trip and fall before I reach the crest,
With little time to say my last goodbyes.

I didn't choose to boast or advertise
My quest to find the truth, and I confessed
I didn't know how far the village lies.

No one would tell me I should recognize
My limitations in the final test,
The futile struggle with my last goodbyes.

The failure in my quest is no surprise—
Too many hurts that haven't been redressed.
I cannot tell how far the village lies,
Because I never said my last goodbyes.

MULBERRY TIME

Someone calls my name.
Outside, a full moon
pierces the mulberry tree
and scraps of a Mozart symphony
jangle from the branches.

In the mulberry tree at night
always there is music
but no berries
and man cannot live
by harmonies alone.

The day, the year, the life
fast-forward on the wall,
a silent panorama.
What has been, has been,
and it was worth living.

She stirs by my side.
I touch her lips and whisper
"It was all good." She smiles
touches my hand
and is adrift again.

The moon is setting.
It calls me. Weightless,
I slip through the branches
and float toward the moon,
a comet trailing symphonies.

EPITAPH OF A PROCRASTINATOR

He died too young
as do we all.

Not a hero, not a martyr, not a saint,
but he too died before his work was done.

He planned to clean the garage this weekend,
sort out thirty years of photographs:
parents, houses, wives, children,
friends, lovers, sunsets, flowers,
people with forgotten names,
enough to fill three albums
bound in brown leather.
Label and remember,
paste and remember.

Next week he would go on a diet,
walk two miles every day,
lose twenty pounds,
get more sleep,
make love to his wife,
write letters to old friends,
tell his children he loves them,
read two years of *National Geographic*,
listen to the *Saint Matthew Passion*.

He leaves behind a cluttered garage,
ten shoeboxes full of photographs,
thirty years of good intentions,
and a few people who loved him
as much as he allowed.

The typefont in this book of poetry is Palatino Linotype. Palitino is based on the humanist fonts of the Italian Renaissance, which mirror the letters formed by a broad nib pen; this gives a calligraphic grace. But where the Renaissance faces tend to use smaller letters with longer vertical lines (ascenders and descenders) with lighter strokes, Palatino has larger proportions, and is considered to be a much easier to read typeface.

Printed on acid free paper.

9 780865 348141